Bits from the Boldt

A collection of poems and
images by:

Jeff Burton

Nov 2010

For Kaitlin
Dream
Believe
Live...
always!
JB

Bits from the Boldt
A collection of poems and Images by:
Jeff Burton
Copyright Jeff Burton 2009
All photographs copyright Jeff Burton 2009
All paintings supplied by Jeff Burton 2009

ISBN #: 978-0-557-16455-4

This book is dedicated to my family, friends and to you the reader, I hope you enjoy it! Thank you.

I would like to thank my loving wife and my 5 great kids for all their support and inspiration in my writing and art.

Without you this wouldn't be here.

I love you all!

A cold room that needs to be Warm

It's a small room
won't take much to warm
to a comfortable place

you don't need to spend long
in there
but multiple visits
throughout time

but the bone chilling cold
prickles your skin as you walk through the door
its icy touch lingering
            uncomfortably

this is a room that should be
warm because the only thing
colder then the air
is the throne
of porcelain
that you must reluctantly sit upon.

Poetry

thoughts half finished
ideas half formed
scribbled down
at a moments notice
some make sense
some are barely
coherent
the pen is my
Isis
searching the shores
of my brain
for the fragments of poems,
her Osiris

Punchin In

work is life

life is work

you punch in

you punch out

you are not

the first

nor the last

just as you

took over (punch in)

for someone (punch out)

someone else will be waiting

to punch in

when you

punch out

Blank

it's a white space
       pure
     untouched
       empty
        and
                    alone
   screaming
            for the
        stroke of
            the paintbrush
   the splash of
                    color
            to change its
                life
                            forever

Refused

with a loud

CLANG

the pearly gates slammed

in my face

despite being a warrior

in Gods army

carrying a sword sharpened

on Gods almighty word

spitting in Lucifer's eye

as I cast him back to Hell

I am the

one

your Heaven

refused

an observation

We've all seen the way
you've looked
d
o
w
n
your nose at us
at our life

your condescending
tone
attitude
your little looks
little remarks
little thoughts
your holier than thou
self induced
delusions
and how you feel
compelled to proclaim
your wisdom
on matters
you know little
to nothing about
your ego filled with a self-fulfilling
artistic nature

but please
don't overfill my
grocery bag
you're
squashing
the bread

I am Not a Criminal

Its words

unspoken

Its images

unseen

Not reading poetry

aloud

is like painting

in the dark

It's a crime against art

Complete

A well spent afternoon
consists of
playing outside with my kids
the wind
strong enough to ruffle the hair
and sway the branches
playfully
but not overpowering
the scene offers the glint of
inspiration
causing pen to dance across the page
the ideas
torn
from the jumble of my minds eye
are rough but one still may see the
spirit
within the writing
once it become
complete

Anarchy in Modern Society

Open hours

no time limits

gravity is a non issue; the skies are not the limit

games, heroes and villains

adventure

backgrounds and locations

change and evolve

every minute something new

all if it fun

not longer just black and white

its shades of grey and

splashes

of every colour

the laughter echoes for miles

everything is real

anything is possible

Explanations and logic be damned

everyone is a superhero

somewhere inside

fighting against the shackles of

high speed society

~A Ripple~

It begins as a drop
a lonely
solitary
drip
into an endless sea
of everything/nothing

yet as this drop drips
breaking the surface
as ripple moves outward
a small wave
to start
but as it touches more and
more it grows
until it is a mighty
tidal wave
crashing down
with the tremendous power
of simple kindness

A Feather

the happiest ideas

twitter

like giddy songbirds

brightly sailing about

the blackest intentions

pick apart the soul

with razor like talons

and piercing beaks

wisdom soars around

the psyche

on the broad wings

of the mighty owl

inspiration dives

through the clutter

like a hawk that's spotted a mouse

a flash so swift, so precise

it's like a bird cage,

my mind,

thoughts

dreams

whispers

flutter about

each as unique as the

feathers

that float out

of my head

and

onto

these

pages

At Gunpoint

BANG!!!

I bolt upright
                in my bed
        sweat pouring
                down my face
        I shakily grab my
                                notebook
and write down the final line I heard
        I really hate when my
                        mind
                takes me hostage
                        to give me inspiration

The paved road

to Heaven's pearly gates I was sent
before my time came my cries
for my sins I must repent
the shining light blinds my eyes

there I stood so full of dread
waited for the judgment to proclaim
the flaming sword to cast off my head
to separate my life from the shame

my soul, not pure or ideal
was not ready for here yet
I inflicted wounds that won't heal
but meant no harm, have no regret

but as I stood there I could tell
the best intentions lead to Hell

I have triplets

again the number three
latches itself to my writing
like a shadow
                              or a specter
trailing throughout my life
groups of three
                    are haunting me

Apparitional

The ancient white moon fills the night sky.

From its place above, the landscape stretches backward through time.

An angry ghost floats as if a feather, its memory filled with a raving, blasphemous truth.

Screaming to the moon it pleads to go back, back to a time before its demise and to show an iron will instead of a glass jaw.

Its cries are in vain as the weather intercedes and the moon turns its back behind the approaching storm clouds.

Disengage

you have an axe to grind

and a huge bone to pick

it is obvious you're not of sound mind

your slope of sanity has gotten too slick

your diseased mind has put you on a rampage

yet I won't give you the satisfaction

when you go off the edge I disengage

I refuse to give you the reaction

try and break me down if you've got the might

your verbal claws dig into me

tear me apart, set the pieces alight

then scatter the ashes through the debris

you paint the world in your distorted view

but I will not waste my hate on you

Extinguished

the flash was intense
          searing heat
                    and blinding light

          and suddenly the people
                    rushing past me
          move faster
                    to
                              and
                                        fro
                    coming
                              and
                                        going
          yet none in the same
                    direction as I

          I find myself lost
                    in a surging sea
                    of people
                    everyone hustling
                    pushing past me
                    the surroundings look familiar
                    yet no face
                              turning with recognition
                                        to mine

          I am drowning
                    in the rushing
                              herd
                                        of moving
                                                  people

          I began to
                    call out
                              shout
                    at everyone around me

demanding recognition
      begging for explanation
      reaching out
            to stop
                      anyone
            passing by

      my hands pass
            through the
            faceless shape
            and my mortal mind
            fully grasps the situation
      with the blinding flash
            of extinguished
                  life

End of the Ice Age

It seems
unbelievable
at first
the subtle increase
in temperature
shifting from deep freeze
to lesser freeze
to just cold

the great white slopes
and crystalline peaks
soften
push back
begin their retreat
in their wake
the barren grasslands
are revealed

and look!

over there

it's the lounge chair
I forgot to put away
in the fall.
It's time for the springtime
treasure hunt
in the yard to begin.

In Dreams

In the fleeting seconds of final memory there was a feeling of ecstasy and euphoria.

The absolute bliss bathed her in a radiant glow.

She rolled in the sheets, feeling the warmth of a passionate evening in her dreams.

She could not help but smile as she kissed her husband awake.

Ever faithful to him, she still relishes in the fact that her brain is a whore.

Inspiration

It started in the littlest toe
and slowly sweeps
into the others
rolling through the
foot and up the legs
gaining speed
and intensity
as it steamrolls
through the abdomen
it thunders across
the heart
and rockets up the arms
until the fireball
of brilliance
collides with the mind
unleashing a magical torrent
of ideas

Masterpiece

The hum of the motor
      buzzing fills the air
          revolutions so fast that it's barely noticeable
      yet the sound is unavoidable

This leads into the sensation
      scraping
          scratching
      across the skin
      as a line is drawn

The needle dances
          as the motor buzzes
      and pigment floods the skin
      as a masterpiece is created
          of flesh and ink

No room to Grow

        try again
do it once
     then
           repeat
      repeat
    repeat
         continue with
the same
      practice makes
             perfect
yet who truly wants to be
             perfect
    when there is
      no room to grow
        in perfection

On the Clock

tickity tickity tock
eight hours left on the clock
the clock strikes eight
the boss is late
tickity tickity tock

tickity tickity tock
six hours left on the clock
the clock strikes ten
a mountain of paperwork again
tickity tickity tock

tickity tickity tock
four hours left on the clock
the clock strikes one
lunch break is done
tickity tickity tock

tickity tickity tock
two hours left on the clock
the clock strikes three
it's time for coffee
tickity tickity tock

tickity tickity tock
no more time left on the clock
the work day is done
it's time for fun
tickity tickity tock

Lost Hope

    they were so

        dazzling bright

this brilliant beacon

        of reflecting light

this pile of bones

        picked perfectly clean

            and the people are terrified

        by what they mean

the travellers now

        frozen in fright

          there is no safety to be

          found here

for they are near

        all hope of flight

is lost in these bones

        so white

One little Thumb

It's the tought
the feeling
the absolute joy
of love
in its purest form
as your hand
                    four tiny fingers
                        and one little thumb
rests peacefully
in mine

Ordinary

my mind wanders off in the dreams of day

where I wish I could disappear

to be able to just fly away

straight through the stratosphere

maybe like Mercury running fast

faster than the speed of light

wouldn't that be a blast

the restraints of time, no longer bite

capes and tights, masks and power beams

sidekicks, team ups and so much more

thwarting an arch enemy's evil schemes

being the hero for all to adore

while some of it could be scary

it would be nice to be more than ordinary

Picnic

he wears a uniform
of black and yellow
and tends to be
an unfriendly fellow
with a buzzing flight
he comes into sight
but beware his stinger bite

So who invited
the wasp?

Simplest Joy

the bright red numbers of the clock
scream out
three
twenty three
am
you awoke in a state
crying and uncomfortable
and I awoke with you
to comfort you
and am rewarded by your tiny
smile
the simplest joy
of a full belly
and a clean bum

Society in a box

four straight sides
            surround us
defining the limits
    forcing everything
into a place
how someone
            somewhere
                  sometime
said it should be
            everything bordered
                        framed
      neat and
                  pristine
            Van Gogh may have had a
            square T.V.
      but his imagination
                  like ours
should know no such limits

Stuffed Paper

The page is blank
a clear slate
not even the
faint blue lines are
visible

The naked
white
screams out
loudly
begging to be covered
filled with colour
with thoughts
with ideas

And here it is
before one realizes it
the page is full
no longer stark naked white
it's stuffed full
like
the Thanksgiving turkey

Supernatural/Superfreak?

The unknown
　　　mysterious
　　　extraordinary
　　　magical

　　　　　　　　　　　　　　　　　　　　　　　　…different
　　　　　　　　　　　　　　　　　　　　　　　　　　new
　　　　　　　　　　　　　　　　　　　　　　　　　　　unique
　　　　　　　　　　　　　　　　　　　　　　　　the unusual

　　　　　　　　　not something seen
　　　　　　　　　　　everyday

miracles　　　　　　　　　　　　　　　　　　　hoaxes
special abilities　　　　　　　　　　　　　　　mental illness
supernatural　　　　　　　　　　　　　　　　superfreak

The Last Whispers

It was a turbulent night
tossing
turning
the chatter
and laughter
getting louder
quieter
then louder again
and finally
as sleep
starts to take hold of him
and the last whispers
drift down the hall
the peacefulness of slumber
envelopes
this happy little boy.

The Opening Notes of Autumn

the grey wind whispers across the sky
clouds drift about
once in a while
blue sky
peeks playfully
out from under the sea of clouds

the air is
cool

not cold enough for long pants yet
but cool enough for the tag along jacket

the grass is soft yet
still green
with hints of yellowing
the odd leaf strays across the path
freshly fallen from the trees

the grey wind whispers across the sky
the departing song of the summer
the opening notes of autumn

The Wait

the wait seems
                    unending
            everyday the
pins
        and
                    needles
            of anticipation
the rush of excitement
            mounting every second
until
        at last
                it's time!
        opening the mailbox
            and
                    discovering
            that the package
            still
                isn't
                    here

third times a charm?

so I find myself
third in line
not a bad place to be
some would say
not too close to the
front
in times of initial problems
but not too far away
in space of a limited supply
yet in the case of
being the third
in a line of spouses
I can't help but
wonder
if there is anyone
waiting behind me

tick meets tock

tick tick tick
hustle, hustle
rush to here
             rush from there
tick tick tick

tock tock tock
trains rush in
             trains rush out
people in
      people off
herds going both ways
tock tock tock

tick tick
everyone has places to go
        not places to be
             but more places to go
tock tock

tick
busy busy
       forward surge
           push to the top
     push   puSH   PUSH
tock

one of these days
       tick   meets   tock
            ground zero
             and no one is ever the same

Tools at Hand

like a blinding
Flash
of lightning
the bolt of
inspiration
rips
through my mind
leaving me frantically
searching
for something to write with
which is why
this is
written
in crayon

Writing

The words
swim
around me
swirling and rushing
flowing over me
bits and pieces
fragments catch my brain

I sit for
hours
absorbing the words
letting my poem
spread
on my
page